Let's find out about . . .

SAVING WATER AND ENERGY

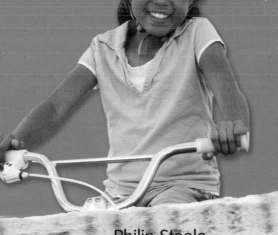

Philip Steele

Tick Tock Books

Studio Manager: Sara Greasley
Editor: Belinda Weber
Designer: Trudi Webb
Production Controller: Ed Green
Production Manager: Suzy Kelly

ISBN: 978-1-84898-089-1
Tracking number: 3374LPP1209

Copyright © *TickTock* Entertainment Ltd. 2010
This edition produced for Scholastic Inc. 2010
First published in Great Britain in 2010 by *TickTock* Entertainment Ltd.,
The Old Sawmill, 103 Goods Station Road, Tunbridge Wells, Kent TN1 2DP, U.K.

Printed in China
9 8 7 6 5 4 3 2 1

Picture credits (t=top; b=bottom; c=center; l=left; r=right; OFC=outside front cover; OBC=outside back cover):
Peter Arnold, Inc./Alamy: 23t. iStock: OFCbr, 4l both, 6, 11t, 13t, 14, 14–15, 15b, 17, 20t, 20b (bin), 21.
Shutterstock: OFCtr, OFCbl, 1, 4c, 4r both, 5, 6–7, 7, 8, 9, 10, 11b, 15t, 16 both, 18–19 all, 20b (girl), 22, 23, 23b,
OBC. Hayley Terry: OFCtl and throughout

Every effort has been made to trace copyright holders, and we apologize in advance for any omissions.
We would be pleased to insert the appropriate acknowledgments in any subsequent edition of this publication.

Contents

Save it!

Do people keep telling you not to waste things around the house? If each one of us started saving instead of wasting, it could make a big difference to our world.

Close the door! You're letting out all the heat!

Turn off the light!

Don't leave appliances on standby!

Turn off the faucet!

What should we be saving?

Water, for a start. Our lives depend on it. We should also use less fuel to heat our homes and drive our cars. Fuels such as oil, gas, and coal are often used to generate electricity. By using less electricity, we can help save these resources.

Forests are important to the health of our planet and should be protected.

Talking Point

Will small changes, such as turning off lights, make a difference?

Yes, small changes can make a difference. If everyone in the world is more careful about how we use our resources, it will help. We need to find ways of protecting our planet's resources before they run out.

Why should we worry about waste?

We use three times more energy than we did 100 years ago, which means that the planet is running out of oil and more forests are being destroyed.

WORD WIZARD!
resources
natural materials such as water, timber, metals, coal, oil, and gas

Precious water

Like all living things, humans need to drink water to survive. We also use water to wash ourselves and to clean our clothes, dishes, houses, and cars.

What else do we use water for?

We use lots of water to help crops grow. Did you know that it takes around 260 gallons (1,000 liters) of water to produce only two pounds (one kilogram) of wheat?

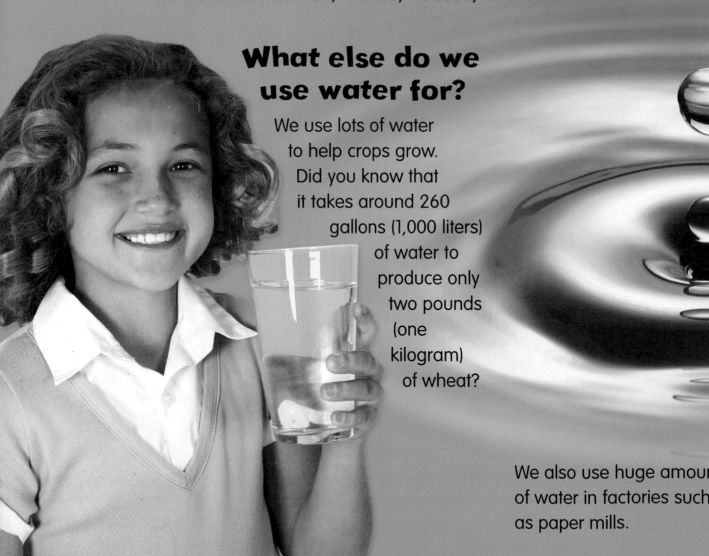

We also use huge amounts of water in factories such as paper mills.

Where does our water come from?

Earth has plenty of water, but most of it is salty seawater, which we can't drink. A lot of it is ice. Only a tiny amount of Earth's water can be easily used by humans.

girl carrying water

Do we have tap water?

In many parts of the world, water isn't piped into people's homes. They have to collect it from rivers or wells. In other countries, water is stored in **reservoirs** and is **filtered** and piped to people's homes.

TALKING POINT

How can I save water?

It's easy to save water. Turn off dripping faucets and take more showers than baths. If you're using hot water, collect the water that runs while you're waiting for it to heat up and then use it to water your plants.

One in four people in the world don't have access to enough clean water.

What is energy?

Energy is the ability to make something work or happen. It is needed every time we start a car or turn on a computer. We can get energy by burning fuels such as wood, plant material, or even garbage. We can dig up reserves of coal, gas, or oil from under the ground.

What happens in a power plant?

In many **power plants**, the heat from fuels is used to turn water into steam. This makes **turbines** spin around and create electricity.

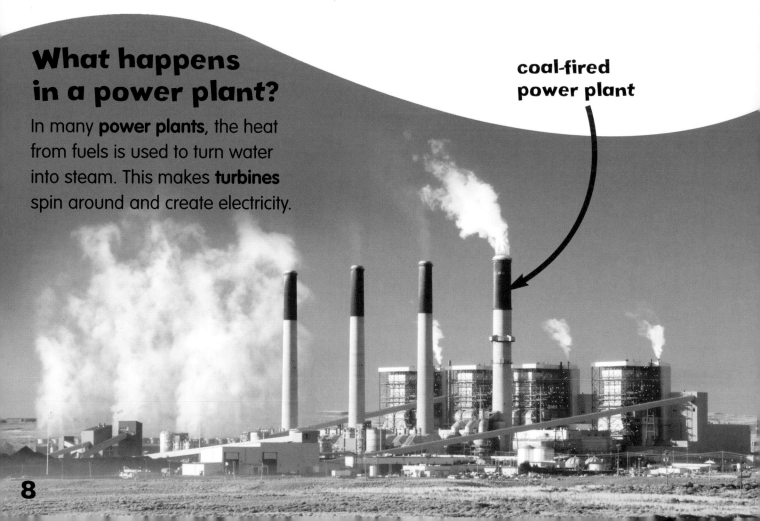

coal-fired power plant

Burning wood produces energy as heat, but the smoke can also cause pollution.

Do fuels affect our planet?

Burning fuels uses up Earth's resources. By using less fuel, we can help save these resources. Some fuels give out gases that **pollute** the air. Nuclear fuel gives out dangerous **radiation**.

Talking Point

How does electricity reach your home from a power plant?

Electricity is fed into your home through cables and wires. The cables are either hung from poles or they run under the ground. Once in your house, smaller wires carry the electricity to your television and other electrical appliances.

WORD WIZARD!

nuclear fuel

a metal such as uranium that changes its structure to produce heat

From land and water

When we burn wood or coal, its energy is used up. Other types of energy can be used again and again. These are called renewable. We can use natural heat from deep inside our planet to generate electricity in some power plants. This is called **geothermal** power.

The center of Earth is boiling hot—so hot that even rocks melt. Geothermal power plants use this heat and turn it into electricity.

dam

rushing water

How can water make power?

Rushing water can be used to turn turbines. This type of power is called **hydroelectric**. The water may come from waterfalls or from dammed rivers.

Talking point

Can we use the ocean to generate electricity?

The tides and currents of the ocean may be used to drive turbines and generate electricity. We can also use the energy from waves. Waves make things bob up and down, and a turbine can use this motion to generate energy.

What is wave power?

Waves form wherever there is wind and water. They are full of energy. Special machines collect this energy and use it to power turbines.

Wind and the Sun

Other forms of natural renewable energy include wind and the Sun. Both are clean and safe to use.

How can we use wind power?

A long time ago, windmills were used to grind grain or pump water. Today, we use them as turbines to generate electricity.

Wind turbines may be set up over large areas called wind farms. Small wind turbines can provide energy for a single house.

Wind turbines can work at wind speeds of between 6–56 mph (10–90km/h).

The Sun has provided Earth with energy for around 4.6 billion years.

How can we use sun power?

The warmth of the Sun provides solar energy. It can be used to provide heat or to generate electricity in power plants.

What are solar panels?

Special panels can be attached to the roofs of buildings. Some panels can be used to heat water in a house. Other panels contain cells that can turn sunlight into useful electricity.

solar panels

Can we save energy at home?

On a cold day, you need to wrap up well to stay warm. You use a layer of clothing to keep in your body warmth. This is called insulation. Houses need insulation, too, so that all of the warmth is held in and not wasted.

How can we keep a house warm?

A double wall keeps a house extra warm. Two layers of glass in windows keep the warmth in. This is called double glazing.

double-glazed window

WORD WIZARD!

insulation
any material that is used to slow down the rate of temperature change

Insulate the attic to stop warmth from escaping through the roof.

energy-saving light bulb

Light bulbs like this have been designed to use less electricty. They last longer, too.

Does insulation make a difference?

In a typical house, almost one half of the warmth is lost through the roof and walls. Good Insulation means that much less energy is used. Using less energy helps save our planet's resources and also saves your family a lot of money.

How can we keep our homes cool?

In hot weather, a house needs to be kept cool. Air conditioners use up a lot of energy. Electric fans use a little less. But best of all is natural **ventilation**. Let the air flow through the building.

Indoor savings

Many of the things we do at home every day use up a lot of energy. So let's change our ways!

How can you stay cozy in bed?

Even if it's chilly, there's no need to leave the heating on overnight. Put an extra blanket on the bed and insulate yourself!

In the bathroom

Don't bathe with the faucet running. Use less water in the bathtub or shower for a shorter time.

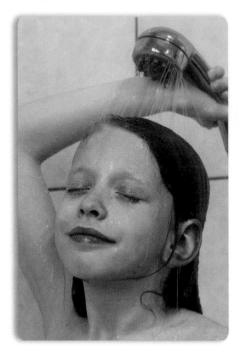

blanket

Washing clothes

Use the energy-saving setting on washing machines. Wash small amounts of clothes by hand. Dry them outside on a clothesline. That way, you won't need to use a dryer!

Saving electricity

Many homes are cluttered with electrical goods such as radios and computers. When they are not in use, turn them off. Don't leave them on **standby**. Some appliances may be fitted with timers to cut down on waste.

turn off the TV

How else can I help save resources?

Think about how you use things around the house. Use a bowl of water for washing the dishes instead of washing them under running water. Put on extra clothes instead of turning on the heat.

Out and about

Walking or riding a bike to school is great exercise. Our own bodies provide the energy to walk and ride. Other ways of getting around burn oil or use electricity. This uses up **valuable** resources.

ride a bike

Exhaust fumes from traffic pollute the air.

How can cars use less fuel?

Some types of cars use up a lot of gas, but others use less. Driving at a regular, moderate speed can save fuel, too. Carpooling uses fewer resources.

WORD WIZARD!
public
transportation
vehicles that carry many people
at once, such as buses
and trains

Talking Point

Why is it good to take buses and trains?

Public transportation burns up fuel, but it carries many people at the same time. If more people take buses and trains, there will be fewer cars on the roads.

How should you spend your leisure time?

Hobbies that don't use up fuel or power, such as gymnastics or ballet, will save energy and keep you in shape and healthy, too. Local vacations will use less fuel than traveling to faraway places.

High-speed trains, such as this Japanese bullet train, mean that more people are likely to use public transportation instead of cars.

19

What is recycling?

Many of the products we use can be made into new materials once they are worn out or used up. The metal from scrapped cars can be used to make new ones. This is called **recycling**.

Scrap metal from old cars can be melted down and used again.

What can we recycle?

We can recycle paper, aluminum cans, glass, plastic, wood, and electrical goods. Some items for recycling may be sorted out and taken out with the trash. We can take other items to recycling centers.

Garden recycling

If you have a garden, you can recycle fruit and vegetable matter into compost.

Compost is just broken-down fruit and vegetable matter that puts the nutrients and richness back into the soil. You can turn fruit and vegetable peels into compost.

Add compost to soil when you plant things.

Talking Point

How do I know what I can recycle?

Many products are marked with a recycling symbol. These products are made from materials that can be used again. Try to take these things to a recycling center near your home.

Can I recycle water?

Yes. Use bath water on your plants. After a bath, leave the water to cool and then collect it in buckets to use on the plants. You can also collect rainwater in containers. Make sure each container has a lid that fits tightly so that animals can't fall in.

Helping the world

Did you know that saving energy and water in your town can help people all around the world? Everyone should try to save energy.

What is global warming?

The fumes from transportation, power plants, factories, and large farms pollute the air. These gases surround the entire planet. They raise the temperature, causing **global warming**.

dried-up riverbed

What is climate change?

Global warming is already changing the world's climates. In the future, some places will become stormier and wetter. Others will become drier and dustier, with little water.

Cleaning the planet

Some organizations work to clean our planet. Others help bring clean water to people. This women is planting a tree. Trees trap moisture in the soil and help clean the air.

When you buy fruit and vegetables, look on the labels to see where they were grown.

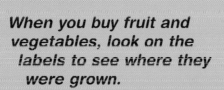

Why should we eat food grown locally?

Supermarkets sell food grown in many different parts of the world. This food has to be transported long distances by truck, ship, or airplane, using a lot of fuel. If we all use less fuel and power, we are helping make the world a cleaner place.

Talking point

What can I do to help the environment?

If you follow the tips in this book, you will be well on your way to helping the **environment**. Be careful when you use electricity or other fuels and try to think about ways you can use less energy. Recycle as many things as you can.

23

Glossary

environment the world around us, including land, sea, air, and living things

filtered having strained and removed impurities from a liquid such as water

geothermal using heat from inside Earth

global warming a rise in the temperature of our planet

hydroelectric providing power generated by the flow of water

pollute to poison land, sea, or air with waste or chemicals

power plant a large factory where electricity is generated

radiation the giving off of rays, such as light or heat. Some of the rays given off by the materials used in nuclear reactions may be dangerous.

recycling processing worn-out or discarded materials so that they can be used again

reservoir a large lake or tank used for storing liquids such as water

standby the setting on an appliance that allows it to be restarted without it having been fully turned off

turbine a spinning motor that is used to generate electricity

valuable of great importance or worth a lot of money

ventilation the passage of air through an enclosed space, such as a house

Index